A FAN'S GUIDE TO UNDERSTANDING THE NFL DRAFT

STRATEGIES, TACTICS, AND CASE STUDIES
FOR BUILDING A PROFESSIONAL FOOTBALL
TEAM

BRUCE IRONS

WOLF MOUNTAIN
- PUBLISHING -

ISBN 978-1-952286-01-8 (paperback)

ISBN 978-1-952286-00-1 (ebook)

"You take the best player."
- Ted Thompson, former Vice President of Football Operations for the Seattle Seahawks and General Manager of the Green Bay Packers

CONTENTS

DEDICATION

Dedicated to the men who risk their lives and physical well-being so we can be entertained on Sundays, and to Andy, Mike, and Dustin for talking to me about it too much.

INTRODUCTION

Do you like football? Do you like watching your team every Sunday in the fall? Do you want a deeper understanding of how your team was built? Do you want to appreciate this great game a little more?

Then this is the guide for you.

We'll cover everything from how the draft works, to themes and strategies that teams use, to specific case studies that help you understand why teams draft the way they do.

We'll put you in the driver's seat so you understand what it's like trying to draft for an NFL team.

This guide is an exploration into draft philosophy, but one of the keys to understanding the draft is to realize that there are no rules and there are no masters. Every rule has an exception, every General Manager has hits and misses.

Bill Walsh was the 49ers GM that drafted quarterback Joe Montana in the 3rd round of the 1979 draft. Montana won four Super Bowls en route to the Hall of Fame and was a member of the NFL 100th Anniversary All-Time Team. Wow, Bill Walsh must have been a genius to find talent like that in the 3rd round, right?

Yes, but 53 picks earlier, he selected James Owens, a wide receiver who only started 6 games before getting cut from the team after two years.

Bill Walsh is a genius, but he took James Owens over Joe Montana.

Oh, but that's not fair because quarterbacks are hard to scout and that was a long time ago.

Then let's consider John Schneider, the Seahawks GM that drafted cornerback Richard Sherman in the 5th round of the 2011 NFL draft. Sherman was one of the best defensive players of the decade, making the All-Pro team five times and leading the NFL in interceptions in 2013.

This makes Schneider a genius, right?

Sure, but 47 picks earlier, he drafted wide receiver Kris Durham, who was cut after only appearing in 3 games and gaining 30 total yards as a rookie.

John Schneider built a Super Bowl champion, but he took Kris Durham over Richard Sherman.

NFL GMs, even the very best, miss on picks all the time.

Quarterback is the most important position in the game, causing teams to reach for them in the draft. Even though quarterbacks are over-drafted, Russell Wilson and Nick Foles fell to the 3rd round, while Tom Brady fell to the 6th. Between them, they won five Super Bowls in a six year stretch, while 1st round picks like Blake Bortles and Johnny Manziel bounced out of the league.

It seems logical that the best players are at the top of

the draft, but Pro Football Focus's 2019 All-Rookie team only had 6 first round picks in their 22 player team.

Do you see the trend?

No one gets this right all the time. There's rarely a clear-cut "right" choice at any pick, but there's usually a whole bunch of wrong choices.

As a fan, this can be maddening.

This guide will help you better understand the philosophies of approaching the draft and why teams do the things they do. It won't tell you what teams "should" do (building a football team and assessing players in the draft is far too complex for that), but it will help you understand how teams process those decisions.

I've found the draft to be one of the most interesting parts of football and I hope this guide helps you understand, appreciate, and (most importantly) enjoy it more.

PART I

ABOUT THE DRAFT

1
——

HOW THE DRAFT WORKS

Football, at its core, is a kids game. It was popular in college long before it was a professional sport, and kids have played some variation of it since the 1200s.

When kids today play football at the park, they choose captains and take turns picking players. That's a lot like the NFL draft, except there's 32 captains and they're all millionaires that work for billionaires.

Every year, players coming out of college subject themselves to the National Football League Draft, where 32 professional teams take turns choosing who they want on their squad. The draft order is set by lining up all the non-playoff teams by record, with the worst choosing first, followed by all the playoff teams in reverse order of finish, with the Super Bowl champion picking last.

The draft has 7 rounds. When the order is initially set, each team has seven picks, all in the same slot each round. In addition to this, the league awards up to 32 compensatory picks (extra picks in rounds 3 through 7 that teams can get if they suffered net losses in free agency the previous year).

This setup lets the worst teams pick first and get the best players... in theory.

I say "in theory" because it's hard to tell which players will be the best.

Extremely hard.

Super-duper, near-impossible, extremely hard.

And even that is an understatement.

Let's just leave it at "the draft is hard."

Teams that do it well reap the benefits and tend to stay good, while teams that draft poorly... don't.

Sure, there are other ways to improve a team, but none is as critical as the draft.

Let's examine why.

WHY THE DRAFT IS SO IMPORTANT

There are many ways to add players to a team, but to understand the importance of the draft, you have to look at it in the context of team goals.

Teams are trying to win a championship. To do so, they're trying to get as many good players as possible. The biggest hurdle to stacking a team with great players? The salary cap.

Teams are limited in the amount of money they can pay their players. Good players can demand a higher salary. Free market economics at work!

The salary cap rules on the NFL are far more strict than those of the NBA or MLB. Sure, teams in the NFL can defer some money forward, and there are ways to distribute cap hits, but the piper always has to be paid.

Prior to the start of the 2020 MLB season, the New York Yankees had a payroll of over $240M, while the Miami Marlins were under $45M. The luxury tax model allows teams to simply outspend other teams in an effort to buy a title.

In the NBA, a similar luxury tax model exists and there are fewer players. With only five players from a team on the court at a time, players often form super-teams, a trend that started when back-to-back MVP LeBron James and four-time All-Star Chris Bosh both decided to join six-time All-Star Dwayne Wade on the Miami Heat in 2010.

In the NFL, there are 22 players on the field at a time and each game is impacted by over 100 players and dozens of coaches. With that many players, it's impossible to make a super team like in the NBA. And with stricter cap rules than MLB, NFL teams simply cannot attempt to buy a championship like they can in baseball.

Building a winning team in the NFL is far more challenging than that.

Within the strict NFL salary cap guidelines, there are three main ways to acquire players: trade, free agency, and the draft.

Let's say you're an NFL GM and you're trying to build a team.

In a trade, you have to give up compensation (usually draft picks, but sometimes other players) to get a player. When you trade for a player, you'll probably want to make sure that player will be around long enough for the team to recoup their investment (because losing value on your investments will not lead to great results). In most cases, this means negotiating a new contract with the player to ensure they stick around.

With free agency, you don't have to give up picks or other players, you just have to offer enough money to entice the player to sign with you (interestingly enough, you have to pay more money than the team that currently has them and has been watching them practice every day). Since free agency gives players the ability to choose the team they want to go to when their contract is up, free agency often turns into a bidding war. If you want to sign a free agent, you likely have to pay more than any other team is willing to pay. That's expensive. That's why free agency usually has way more losers than winners.

In the draft, however, you just get to pick a player you want and they're automatically on your team. The best part is that the NFL Collective Bargaining Agreement gives rookies a "slotted" salary (which is lower than the going rate for free agents) based on where they were selected. Rookie contracts are all for a standard four-year term (plus teams get a fifth-year option for first round picks).

So the options are to pay more money than any other team will pay to sign a player in free agency, give up picks and/or players (and probably a new contract) to trade for a player, or get a free player at an artificially low fixed-rate salary through the draft.

When you look at it like that, it's clear why the draft is so important. Young, cheap players are a great way to build a football team.

In many regards, trades and free agency are only necessary when teams have failed at the draft.

Make no mistake, though, every team, every GM, fails

at the draft in some regard. This is one of the most challenging jobs in sports and no one ever gets it right every time.

Did I mention that it's really hard?

3

WHY THE DRAFT IS SO HARD

I f you take nothing away from this book except one
thing, make it this:

Drafting is hard.

Drafting is hard for a lot of reasons, but the biggest
challenge is simply projecting how a player will play in
the pros after watching him play in college.

With free agency and trades, you've already seen how
a player will perform against other pros. It's a different
scheme and a different city, but it's a much better indi-
cator than any evaluations you can make on kids in
college, and you already know that they can stand up to
the mental and physical rigors of the pro game.

Consider that NFL players can stay with the same
team across multiple decades. Successful NFL coaching
staffs implement their systems over many years,
constantly maturing them over time.

College teams, on the other hand, are built through

recruiting. High school players come to a college, practice for a year or two, play for a year or two, and then they're gone. This means that college coaching staffs need to implement much simpler plays and schemes. They have to be picked up and understood by young kids who can use them immediately (and have greater limits on practice time). Just about the time a college player gets proficient in their college scheme, they leave.

This also makes player evaluations more difficult. Just because a kid can understand a basic offense in college doesn't mean he will be able to pick up on the detailed nuances of a pro scheme. Even when college teams run a "pro style" offense, the finer points and deep nuances that come from running and maturing a scheme like that for a decade never get implemented in the college game.

There's also the physical evaluation. Just because a college player is physically dominating in college on Saturdays doesn't mean that he'll be able to dominate in the NFL on Sundays.

In college, you have some fully grown men, upwards of 300 pounds in many cases, trained and primed to join the NFL as some of the best athletes in the world. And in many college games, those dynamos are lining up against wide-eyed 18-year-old kids fresh out of high school who are still growing.

The LSU Tigers won the NCAA National Championship following the 2019 season. They were a powerhouse that will probably have more than a dozen players drafted in the upcoming 2020 draft.

They opened their season with a 55-3 dismantling of

Georgia Southern University (not to be confused, in any way, with the Georgia Bulldogs, the powerhouse school in the state). Georgia Southern University, who squeaked out double and triple overtime wins against teams like South Alabama and Coastal Carolina en route to a loss against Liberty University in the FBC Mortgage Cure Bowl, isn't known as a juggernaut in college football, so don't feel bad if you didn't recognize those names.

In that game, Georgia South had a 5'11" 190-pound freshman quarterback making his first start. His top wide receiver was a 5'10" 170-pound freshman.

By comparison, LSU's Quarterback was potential #1 overall NFL pick, Joe Burrow, a 6'4" 220 pound senior and reigning Heisman Trophy winner. His leading receiver was 6'3" Justin Jefferson, a junior so talented that he is leaving college a year early to declare for the NFL draft, where he is projected by many to go in the first round.

The gap in size, skills, and maturity can be staggering in the college game.

So how can you judge players to see if they're ready for the NFL when they're playing against competition like that? How can you judge if a player lining up against kids who will never make the pros will be successful trying to block TJ Watt or tackle Derrick Henry?

It ain't easy.

So how do they do it?

NFL teams start with a General Manager who typically has final say in all player acquisition moves, including the draft (subject to owner approval, of course). One of the key roles under the GM is Director of College

Scouting, who is tasked with understanding the talent levels and ratings of every college football player in the country (or anywhere else in the world, for that matter).

Since there are literally thousands of draft eligible players each year, Directors of College Scouting typically have a team of people under them, with a hierarchy of national and regional scouts accountable for watching players from different areas. These roles are in addition to assistants, coordinators, and technology analysts that assist the scouts in their duties.

It's a big job with lots of people dealing with a lot of difficult scenarios.

DIFFICULT SCENARIOS

As if scouting players in the college game to try to figure out which ones will perform well in the pro game wasn't hard enough, there's an endless list of scenarios that can make things even more difficult.

These are all things that pop up behind-the-scenes and most fans don't even consider, but they make the task of drafting an NFL team incredibly difficult.

Last Minute Information

Your team has targeted a guy in the first round. He's everything you want at a position of need and then, just an hour before they draft, you learn that he has a heart defect of unknown severity. He's apparently had it his whole life, and there's a second test that might just clear the whole thing up, but the results aren't in yet.

The picks go by and he falls to you. You're not sure if you still want him, though. You scramble through your board and mock scenarios and you have a clear cut number two choice. With three minutes left on the clock, you're about to make your decision when your assistant taps you on the shoulder and shows you a tweet on his phone: there's a rumor that your second choice just hit a woman. Now what do you do?

Only two minutes left on the clock.

Tick, tock...

The Snipe

You were the only team that even showed up to Pro Day at Backwater U in Nowheresville and you just knew the next John Randle was hiding there.

You need a defensive tackle bad, but you're so confident that you can get your guy from Backwater U in the 6th round that you pass up at least four chances to get other good defensive tackles to focus on other needs.

Three slots before your turn, your division rival snags him. There are no more defensive tackles you're even remotely interested in, and all the good free agents signed with other teams last month.

But you need a new starter.

Now you're on the clock... what are you going to do?

The Leak

You put together a great board. You did extra research on the needs and draft tendencies of all the other teams and you already know exactly who you're taking each round. No one's gonna take your guys!

But they do.

The same team, two slots ahead of you, keeps taking the player you want every single round.

You're flabbergasted, scrambling to find a new player on short notice each time your pick comes up. And you can't understand how this is happening... until months later.

Remember that regional scout that got all sassy and threw a steaming hot coffee in your face back in November? Like a good leader, you kept your cool and calmly explained to him that wasn't acceptable behavior and he went back to work.

You dealt with his nonsense because his contract was up in May and you needed his scouting reports to get through the draft. Little did you know that he took a copy of your draft board and all your research over to the team that picked two spots ahead of you.

In June that team announced your old scout as their new personnel director - he was feeding them your inside information the whole time and you had no idea.

Think this doesn't happen? Do you really think people aren't cutthroat in a glamorous business with very scarce, highly sought-after jobs?

The Misleader

You've heard it from two separate sources that a certain player has a certain issue that pretty much removes him from your board. No one else knows, they assure you, but they're good friends and they want you to make a fully informed decision.

Or so they say.

What if the GM who picks after you was paying people to feed you false information? What if they were feeding false information to the three teams ahead of you, too, making sure the player fell to them?

This is a multi-billion dollar business and people are playing to win. You never know who you can trust (which is one of many reasons why nepotism is so prevalent in NFL hiring circles).

Owner Issues

Your turn is up and there's a guard you want. You're convinced that this guy is the next Quenton Nelson and you're pumped to get him on your team.

Then the owner walks in. He sits on the board of a Fortune 100 company and one of the other board members went to Big State U and he really, really likes their wide receiver. The owner doesn't care if no one is projecting him until the 2nd round, he doesn't want to take a chance–you better get him in the first round!

Now what?

If you take the receiver and he flops, then the owner blames you, you get fired, and everyone calls you stupid, making it difficult to ever get a comparable job in this business. If the receiver is good, but the guard is way better, you still look bad - even though you were right!

Or maybe your owner isn't that specific in his meddling. Maybe after you carefully comb through hundreds of players and rank them precisely with 20 other scouts, and have found the perfect defensive lineman for your new scheme, the owner comes in and says he thinks the team really needs to upgrade its safeties and he wants to see results.

Just Randomness

Your team has two major needs, defensive tackle and linebacker, so you trade up to get two 1st round picks. Now you're in a great position to fill your two biggest holes!

When your first pick comes up, there's five defensive tackles you really like, but only one linebacker. Your second pick is just eight slots away, so of course you take that one linebacker, right? One of those defensive tackles will fall... right?

Right after your pick, a run starts on defensive tackles. In the eight picks before your next selection, all five defensive tackles you like get picked. Later you learn that no one was going to take a Linebacker for another two rounds.

Does that make you a terrible GM?

All of these things happen and more.

The number of hurdles that emerge during the draft process is just staggering.

It's nearly impossible to accurately "know" that you are making the right pick at any point in the draft.

A few years ago, there was a great story about why the Browns made the terrible decision to draft future bust Johnny Manziel in the first round: a homeless guy told Browns owner Jimmy Haslam to draft him.

Talk about random!

PART II

STRATEGIES AND TACTICS

4

OVERVIEW

Most teams don't just listen to what random homeless strangers tell them to do in the draft.

Most teams put together a plan and a strategy. They focus on what they want their team to be, they define an identity, and then they draft players that fit that identity.

A team built around a wide open passing attack won't place high value on a bruising, road-grading running back, but a team that wants to control the clock and grind teams down will.

Many people ask "Why not both?"

Why not have a wide open passing attack and a power running attack?

For starters, it's counter-productive. If you have a great quick-strike passing attack, why slow it down with a power run game? On the flip side, if you're overpowering a defense with a steam-rolling run game, why would you stop to start throwing passes?

The type of offensive line personnel you would need for that kind of passing attack would be completely different than what you would need for a power run game, too.

Are there linemen who can do both? Sure, but there aren't many and they don't come cheap. Whether you draft them, sign them as free agents, or trade for them, acquiring five of them would take so many resources that you probably wouldn't be able to field a complete team.

But if you just want to find five guys who are power run blockers or five guys who are agile pass protectors, things get exponentially easier.

This is why teams create an identity and then add players that fit that identity.

It's one of the hard realities of building a football team: you can't be good at everything.

5

YOU CAN'T BE GOOD AT EVERYTHING

Y ou know what's hard?
       Being an astronaut. It takes a lot of time and
       training.

You know what else is hard?

Being a brain surgeon. You have to really know a lot about the human body and have steady hands. Oh, being a mechanic is hard, too, so is being a radio control tower operator - it's like the most stressful job in the world - and driving a forklift is tougher than it sounds.

Do you have any of these jobs?

Do you have all of them?

No? Why not?

Because they're all hard and being good at everything is hard.

For some reason, though, fans seem to expect their GM to get great players at every position.

I'm sorry, but that's just not how football works. In football, you need to create a team identity and then try to build around that. Look back at some of the recent Super Bowl champions and you can see the need for an identity.

The 2020 Chiefs had a high-flying passing attack capable of erasing double-digit deficits in each of their three playoff games.

The 2016 Denver Broncos were built on a smothering defense and had an offense led by a far-past-due Peyton Manning leading them to just enough points through veteran savvy and little else.

The 2012 Giants were built on a punishing defensive front and a complimentary run game of bowling ball Brandon Jacobs and pinball Ahmad Bradshaw.

The Patriots dynasty was built around having an efficient offense and an adaptive defense that focused on game-planning to take away the opponents top weapons. They didn't always have great receivers, offensive line, and edge rushers, but they had a chameleon-like identity.

Before you get into draft strategy, you need to decide what your team's identity is. This will determine what kind of players you'll draft.

If you want a defense that focuses on stopping the pass, look for linebackers that can run with tight ends and play zone coverage. If you want a defense that focuses on stopping the run, look for skull-thumping linebackers that don't get pushed around.

The first type of defense will require a line of quick, penetrating rushers. The second type will need big, gap-filling run stuffers. Units need complementary players.

You can't be good at everything and if you don't have a focus, your team won't be a coherent symphony, it will be a jumbled mess.

Teams do their best to be balanced, of course. No team tries to get good at one thing while completely ignoring the other, but even with the best efforts, seemingly complete and dominant teams can fall short. The 2018 Rams team had a great (and expensive) defense paired with a record-breaking offense. Their defense held the Patriots to a mere 13 points (the only time the Patriots scored less that season was when they played the Lions, coached by Matt Patricia, who understood the Patriots inside-out as their former Defensive Coordinator).

Even with that remarkable defensive performance, the Rams still couldn't win. After topping 20 points in 12 of their 16 regular season games, they could only manage 3 measly points in the Super Bowl. Their weakness? Defensive audibles. As good as their offense was, they couldn't adapt when the Patriots changed their defensive play every single down.

The 2016 Falcons looked good at everything. A pinball offense and one of the fastest defenses the league had ever seen. They looked unstoppable.

Well, they looked unstoppable all the way up to their famous 28-3 3rd quarter Super Bowl lead, anyway. That was when the Patriots found the Falcons weakness: stamina. That speedy defense that ran around smothering everything couldn't keep up as the Patriots went with a fast-paced offense that focused on short plays. They ran 93 plays (more than twice as many as the Falcons ran), completely gassed the Falcons defense, and won the game in overtime.

The 2012 49ers looked unstoppable, too. They had a

punishing physical defense and a new-age offense led by dual-threat quarterback Colin Kaepernick. They averaged over 30 points per game in the playoffs, but couldn't keep pace with the big play capabilities of the Ravens, who scored a touchdown in two-and-a-half minutes on their first drive, got another touchdown on a drive that took only nine seconds before the half (thanks to a 56 yard pass), and answered the 49ers field goal to end the first half with a 108-yard kickoff return for a touchdown to start the second half.

The 2011 Packers looked like they had an offense that would just simply outscore everyone all the way through the Super Bowl after going 15-1, but their defense just couldn't keep up and the Giants dropped 37 points to knock them out of the playoffs.

The 2007 Patriots sure looked unstoppable, starting off 18-0 on their way to the Super Bowl, but the Giants (who had lost to the Patriots just a few weeks earlier) showed that any team really can beat any other team on any given Sunday.

All teams have weaknesses, no matter how good they are at what they do.

Go back further to the 1996 Packers, who looked like one of the most dominant teams of all time when they ranked number one in the league in scoring offense and number one in the league in scoring defense to go along with the number one ranked special teams unit in the league. They won the Super Bowl and looked like they were the best at everything. That team lost three games that season (including one to the Chiefs, who didn't even make the playoffs), proving that even if you look great at everything, no team is unstoppable.

All of these examples just go to show how hard it is to put together a winning team.

There are 32 teams, all taking different approaches to building their team, coaching their players, and planning for games and they're all competing for the same thing: the one Lombardi Trophy that gets handed out at the end of each year.

You have to pick a strategy to try to win with.

Do you want a tough defense complemented by a power running game like the 2013 Super Bowl champion Seahawks or do you want a big-play passing attack complemented by big special teams plays like the 2012 Super Bowl champion Ravens? Or maybe you want a versatile offense that doesn't dominate, but finds ways to grind out points complemented by a savvy defense that can adapt to stymie many different offensive styles like the 2019 Super Bowl champion Patriots?

There's no right answer, but you have to pick one.

If you look at how your favorite team has drafted over the last five years and play close attention to how their offense and defense have deployed their plays, you can get a better understanding of what their strategy is and how they may approach the draft.

6

PLAYER EVALUATION

Once you know what kind of team you want to build, you have to start evaluating the thousands of draft-eligible college players to determine which ones you want to pick.

How do you evaluate all those players?

With your team of trusted scouts, of course!

For the most part, scouts watch college football games to determine how good they think players are. After all, what better way to judge how good someone is at playing football than by watching them play football?

Scouts from each NFL team are typically assigned to regions to watch all the players in a certain geographic area. During the season, they are on the road non-stop, going from game to game to see as many players as possible and make their evaluations.

When they aren't at games, they're at practices or at their hotel watching film and writing reports or meeting with coaches, trying to get more inside information. Relationship-building becomes a big part of scouting.

College coaches look good when their players go pro, so they're doing everything they can beyond just coaching them well. They're advertising their players and lobbying for them. However, they can't just tell a scout that every player they have is a hidden gem or a future dynamo because the scout would stop believing them after the first couple of times.

When a coach gives scouts good, honest insight (such as a player who really looks like he would break out if he could stay healthy or a guy whose performance dipped for understandable - and temporary - circumstances), it increases the likelihood that the scout will listen, which increases the likelihood that the player will get drafted, which increases the likelihood of a strong, continued scout-coach relationship.

These types of trusted relationships can take years to develop. When a college coach has a good relationship with a pro scout, it's no coincidence when that pro team gets a lot of players from that school.

When scouts are evaluating college players, there's an endless list of things to consider, including:

- How will this player make the jump from college, where he's playing against 18-year-old kids right out of high school, to the pros, where he'll face the most freakish physical athletes in the history of the world when they all want to inflict pain on him?

- How will this player fit into the team's scheme? Can that receiver who only ran stop routes and crossing patterns in college go deep at the pro level? He ran a 4.39 at the Combine, so why didn't he ever go deep? Can that gap-shooting defensive lineman really hold up in a two-gap system? He has the size, so why didn't his college coach ask him to do that?
- How will this player's body grow as he reaches physical maturity? How will his outlook and work ethic evolve over time? What about his ego? Don't forget that each of these guys has been "the man" their whole life and is used to everyone fawning over them... something that won't happen if you pick him on the last day of the draft.
- How will this player's injury history play out in the future? Were those college injuries freak occurrences or a sign of things to come?

These are very hard questions to answer. This is why teams dig deep into a player's background before selecting him. They talk to family, friends, old coaches, old rivals, team doctors, anyone they can get to talk.

Aside from all this, there's the matter of game film.

Most players in college, even if they are in school 4 or 5 years, typically only start for a season or two.

This limits the amount you can actually study a player. There's only a dozen games each year, and sometimes a player misses some due to injury.

Sometimes there's a bowl game at the end of the year for another opportunity to see a guy play, but more often than not, draft prospects are sitting them out to save their bodies and avoid an injury prior to being drafted.

This can call into question about how much a player is dedicated to the game. As it becomes more common, it is more acceptable (especially when established pro players are sitting out entire preseasons), but it is still a missed opportunity to see a player in game action one more time.

Live games are the best way to evaluate a player, but there are a couple other key events that weigh heavily into college player evaluation: the Senior Bowl and the Scouting Combine.

THE SENIOR BOWL

The regular season games are one of the best places to get an evaluation on players. You can watch them week in, week out against a variety of opponents and a variety of gameplans. This is where you can see how a receiver who slices through zone coverage reacts to press man and how a quarterback adapts to different types of defenses.

But as we discussed earlier, one of the big challenges with this is that college competition isn't always that tough.

That's why we have the Senior Bowl.

The Senior Bowl is a scrimmage where the top senior prospects can showcase their skills against the best competition in the country after the season is over.

Ok, now we're talking; let's see how the best seniors in the nation match up against each other!

But, still, it's only one game. A lot can happen in one game. Maybe a player has a bad day or maybe he just doesn't get a lot of reps or sprains an ankle - can so much ride on one game?

Kind of.

Scouts actually get their best Senior Bowl insights from the practices leading up to the game. That's where scouts can see all the one-on-one matchups and drills. How does that receiver with a smooth release respond in drills against the best press corners in the class? How does that power-rushing defensive tackle fare against the biggest offensive tackles coming out?

Senior Bowl practices provide these insights. In fact, most scouts don't even watch the game, they leave as soon as the last practice finishes (after they have some drinks with the other scouts, of course).

In 2020, defensive tackle prospect Javon Kinlaw actually chose not to participate in the game, letting a week of dominant Senior Bowl practices speak for themselves. Time will tell if it works out for Kinlaw, but history shows that guys who dominate Senior Bowl practices tend to have pretty good careers. Some notable Senior Bowl practice stars from the recent past include Aaron Donald and Deebo Samuel.

Aaron Donald was a productive player in college but caught a bad rap for being undersized. After his senior year, he was viewed as a mid-round pick who could possibly slip until Day 3.

Then he went to the Senior Bowl.

In every practice, he was unstoppable and unblockable.

That was enough to convince the Rams to take him with the 13th overall pick. He was an All-Pro five times in his first six seasons and won Defensive Player of the Year twice.

Deebo Samuel was an undersized receiver who was kind of lost in the wash as a probably Day 3 pick with a niche skill set.

Like Aaron Donald, he flashed his skills in Senior Bowl practice, showing an impressive release and great route running while proving to be pretty much unguardable by any defensive back in attendance.

He moved up draft boards and was selected in the 2nd round by the 49ers, becoming a key member of their Super Bowl team and garnering a spot on everyone's All-Rookie Team.

While players who do well at Senior Bowl practices tend to have good careers, the opposite can also be true.

The same year that Aaron Donald was tearing up Senior Bowl practices, Quarterback Tajh Boyd was struggling.

A 3-year starter at Clemson and First Team All American in 2012, Boyd looked like he might have a bright future in the NFL. Despite being undersized (though taller than Russell Wilson and Kyler Murray), he was productive and left college as Clemson's all-time career leader in passing yards and touchdowns.

Scouts showed up to watch him at Senior Bowl practices and were not impressed. Boyd slipped to the 6th round, but he couldn't even make a roster out of training camp. He played a season for the Boston Brawlers of the Fall Experimental League, then failed to stick with a couple of Canadian Football League teams. His career was over in relatively short order.

The Senior Bowl practices predicted all of this. It's not infallible, but it's one of the best indicators for how college prospects match up against premier talent.

Unlike some other measurables, there's no way to fake being good at the Senior Bowl.

THE SCOUTING COMBINE

The Scouting Combine is an event at the end of February where you can get all the measurables on the top draft-eligible players. How many times can they bench press 225 pounds? How fast can they run the 40 yard dash? How quick can they do a 3-cone drill?

These can be helpful indicators of how athletic a player is. In ye olden days, the Combine was just a chance for scouts to see how players measured up. This was intended to just be a helpful supplemental measure to complement all the game film as a part of player analysis.

But players aren't stupid (at least their agents aren't) - they will train specifically for the Combine.

That means that linemen will work specifically on increasing their bench press so they can get a better strength rating. It also means that skill position players and defensive backs will work on their 40 times by focusing on their sprinter stance, their jump out of the blocks, and their arm and chest mechanics when they are sprinting in a straight line wearing track shoes.

As you can imagine, this may not transfer to game speed for a wide receiver running through the snow while a physical cornerback is jamming him at the line. The original idea behind the 40-yard dash was just to have players run and see who was faster, but as time went on, players focused more on doing well on the drill rather than being "football fast."

We all know that these drills aren't perfectly aligned to real life game conditions, but when players start to show flashy measurables, scouts sure can get tempted.

History is full of workout warriors who excelled at the Combine far more than they ever excelled on the field, prompting scouts to wonder if the player is just a gold-mine of untapped potential.

More often than not, it isn't.

Defensive end Mike Mamula is the poster child for workout warrior syndrome. He had a nondescript college career with no real accolades beyond a yawn-worthy spot on the 1994 All Big East team. However, Mike was ahead of the curve in understanding the importance of the Combine.

Today, most players do Combine-specific training, but that wasn't always the case.

Mamula is credited for being the first player ever to focus explicitly on training for the Combine drills. His bench press was great and his vertical jump and 40 time were both off the charts for a defensive end. Teams were impressed and he skyrocketed up draft boards, eventually getting drafted 7th overall by the Eagles in 1995, who actually traded up to get him.

Mamula played for the Eagles for five years, never living up to the hype and potential he showed at the Combine and certainly never outshining Hall of Famer Warren Sapp, who was selected five picks later. His on-field performance as a pro player was far more reminiscent of his on-field performance as a college player than it was of his Combine measurables.

This is usually the case.

Matt Jones was a 6'6" 240 pound quarterback at the University of Arkansas. He wasn't a phenom, but had great size for the position and showed his athleticism by setting the SEC record for rushing yards by a QB.

Then at the 2005 Combine, he ran a 4.37 40 - blazingly fast - prompting scouts to wonder if he could play wide receiver. Based primarily on a big frame and a great 40 time (and absolutely zero experience playing wide receiver), the Jaguars drafted him at number 21 overall (ahead of wide receivers like All-Pro Roddy White and three-time Pro-Bowler Vincent Jackson).

Jones played four years, averaging a modest 550 yards per season, and never becoming a true receiving threat. Scouts knew he'd never played the position, but they saw great Combine numbers and let themselves believe that meant he could be a great wide receiver. A decade and a half later, he's still considered a prime example of a player that scouts totally whiffed on because they believed his Combine numbers more than his game film.

The Combine should be used to answer lingering

questions. It should not be considered a holistic evaluation of a player.

It's just additional data.

The Scouting Combine, along with the Senior Bowl and college games give scouts a lot of information on a player, but that's just part of the equation. Things get a lot tougher when you aren't evaluating a single player, but looking at each pick in terms of the value you can get out of the entire draft class.

7

COMMON DRAFT STRATEGIES

W hen you build a team, you don't just have to define what kind of team you want to be, you also have to define a draft process, some sort of guiding principles on how you will approach your draft selections.

Whenever this topic comes up, the "Draft and Develop" approach invariably surfaces. I can't really call Draft and Develop a true "strategy" because it's really more of a common practice that every team has to employ.

Simply put, Draft and Develop means that a team drafts players knowing that they aren't finished products. Everyone wants a blue chip stud that is just going to walk onto the field and dominate from day one, but that hardly ever happens.

Even the best rookies to come out each year struggle to make the Pro Bowl, let alone be an All-Pro as a rookie.

If a player makes it past the first or second round, it's a shaky proposition that they even start as a rookie.

Teams have to develop their players. The only question is to what degree teams value players who are ready to be immediate contributors as opposed to guys with more potential, and how high they will draft the latter.

This is more of a preference that will influence how a team plays out their strategy.

There are three basic, popular strategies, but there is rarely a cut-and-dried straight answer that comes out of either of them. They're vague guidelines more than hard and fast rules and there's a lot of gray around them.

DRAFT FOR NEED

Drafting for need is pretty much what it says: look at the biggest needs your team has and start grabbing players to fill those holes.

In most circles, "drafting for need" has a very negative connotation. In many ways, it's looked at as the fool's path, a desperate plight. It's so derided that the snobbiest of draft snobs will actually insult a GM for taking a player at a position where they need a player.

"Can you believe that guy? They needed an offensive tackle, so he just went ahead and took the best offensive tackle he could find. Puh, what an idiot."

Here's the deal: if the weakest link on your team is offensive tackle and you draft an offensive tackle, while there are better cornerbacks and linebackers on the board, you may be missing the big picture.

It may feel like you are improving your team, but if

you are missing out on a better player, you may be lowering your team's long-term potential to succeed.

BEST PLAYER AVAILABLE

The antithesis of drafting for need. Don't worry about what you think your team's "needs" are, just worry about getting the best players on your team and figure out the rest later.

This is the fallback line for many GMs and fans: "just take the best player available."

It sounds so simple. When the time comes to make a pick, the team should just take the best player on the board, regardless of position or anything else.

Teams that are truly married to BPA would take a wide receiver if a wide receiver was the best player on the board - even if they have two Pro-Bowl wide receivers on the roster already. If they need a linebacker more than anything else, but the best player on the board is a safety, they would take the safety.

It's a simple philosophy, but the implementation is more complex than it seems (we'll get into those challenges a little later).

BEST VALUE AVAILABLE

If you think about a team in the economic sense, where each player has a relative value and a relative utility, and you try to maximize those things on your team, you get closer to the best value philosophy.

Let's say your team's biggest need is wide receiver, but the best player on the board is a running back.

What do you do?

The best player available approach says to just take the running back, but the best value approach takes more factors into consideration.

Let's add a little more information to this equation. We've already established that the best player on the board is a running back and the biggest need is a wide receiver. Let's also say that the team's second-biggest need is linebacker. Add to that the fact that there's only one linebacker worth a lick left on the board, while there are twelve more wide receivers that you think could have a positive impact on your team and the top five remaining running backs are all about equal.

This is where the concept of value comes in.

Every team will balance scarcity and value differently and it will drive their choices.

This is also where trades come in.

Think about it: if all teams valued everything the same way, there would never be any trades.

And if you're drafting for need or you're drafting best player available, trades never really come into the conversation. Trades come in when you're looking for value and they only happen when teams value things differently.

Is Julio Jones worth a couple first-round picks and a few other selections to boot? The Falcons thought so. The Browns didn't. They value things differently.

One of the best examples of value-based maneuvering in recent memory is what the Packers pulled off in the 2018 draft. Holding the 14th overall spot, the Packers needed secondary help and there were a couple good options on the board in Derwin James and Jaire Alexander.

The Packers could have drafted either of those guys and improved their team.

The Saints valued things differently. They were in love with defensive end Marcus Davenport and offered the Packers their 1st round pick at number 27 overall, plus their 5th round pick, *and* their 1st round pick the following year.

As much as the Packers wanted James and Alexander, the value of picking up another 1st round pick was just too much to pass up and they made the deal.

But they didn't stop there.

Once Derwin James went off the board at 17, the Packers made a trade with the Seahawks, sending their 3rd and 6th round picks to move up from 27 to 18 (and gain an extra 7th round pick).

With the 18th pick, they selected Jaire Alexander, one of the players they wanted at 14.

In the end, the Packers had a couple guys they wanted at their spot, so they traded down, waited, then traded back up to get one of them, and picked up an extra 1st round pick in the process.

This is a textbook example of drafting for value.

8

HOW TEAMS USE DRAFT STRATEGIES

W hile value is always at the forefront of draft decisions, it's hard to ignore needs or look away from the best player available.

The truth of the matter is that all of these ideas come together to drive decisions when it's actually time to pick.

So how do teams actually go about this?

RANK GROUPINGS

Teams almost always start with ranking the top 400 or so players, but they don't just have players ranked from 1 to 400.

Doing so would require scoring each player out to three decimal points (or more) and making decisions on details so granular that they probably wouldn't matter. Would you really take a tight end with a 7.643 rating over a safety with a 7.642 rating just because the number was higher?

Would you even believe your own rankings to that level of detail?

Teams are smart enough to know that they can't accurately grade players to that level of detail, so not only would rating players to that degree be a waste of time, it would also make any decisions based on that information counter-productive.

Instead, teams tend to rank the players in tiers. Those tiers aren't necessarily broken out into groups of 5 or 10 or even 32 - they're broken out by relative perceived talent of the players in the draft pool.

After looking at all the players, a team may judge the talent and come out with an ultra-elite tier with three players at the very top followed by a tier of four elite players and then a tier of nine very good players before a group of 20 guys that they think are around the same level of talent.

That means that if this team picks 8th, they're really going to hope one of those seven ultra-elite or elite players falls. This can happen if other teams rank the players differently or if one of those teams needs a high-profile position like quarterback and takes a player that isn't as good, because they really need a guy at that position (remember when we talked about drafting for need? The most common occurrence is when a team needs a quarterback).

By the same token, if a team with those same rankings is drafting at 22, they see how low the odds are that they get someone from that group of 16 players in their top three tiers. They would probably be pretty open to trading back up to 14 spots, allowing them to gain an extra pick while still getting a player of the same perceived impact from their fourth tier.

TARGET BOARDS

Once teams have their tiers set, they put together their target board.

This is that big grid that you see in the background of Instagram pictures of the draft rooms that has all the names blurred out.

All the available player positions make up the columns on the top and all the draft rounds make up the columns. Then, all the players the team is targeting end up in boxes, giving them a broad view of available players and when they think they would take them.

This is also where positional value starts to come into play.

9

POSITIONAL VALUE

N ot all positions are created equal. Punters, for example, are a position you hope you never even have to use.

Quarterback, on the other hand, is, without question, the most important position in the game. Not only do they touch the ball every play, it might be the hardest position to play in sports.

QUARTERBACKS

What makes Quarterbacks so hard to find?

First, it's hard to throw the ball 60 yards, and even harder to do it accurately. Now, think about how hard it is to hit a guy 60 yards away in stride while he's running with 4.37 speed *and* has a guy who is just as fast running so close beside him that their hips are almost touching.

Then imagine doing this while 6'3" monsters are pushing straight at you, waving their hands and jumping up and down to block your view and the ball. Oh, and there's a 6'5" guy who runs a 4.8 40 yard dash coming from behind you - where you can't even see - trying to bury his helmet into your spine (don't worry, he'll make it look like an accident).

While all this is going on, the quarterback needs the mental processing speed to read the play adjustments for a call like Strong Blue Left 17 Shift Heavy Z Sluggo Y Switch (unless it's an audible) when every one of his five receiving options can change his assignment or route based on how the 11 defenders are playing in the span of about 2.5 seconds.

It's not as easy as it sounds.

This is why QBs are so hard to find.

So you have an incredibly difficult position to play and it also happens to be the most important position in the game. A team can't really win with a bad one, so teams are desperate and often *knowingly* make foolish decisions to try to get one.

PREMIUM POSITIONS

Quarterback is the most important position in the game of football, but it is a team game, so what's the next most important position?

Well, that's up for debate. This is where you get into maxims like "defense wins championships" and "the game is won and lost in the trenches."

In my analysis of the game and drafting trends, there are four positions directly below quarterback that are more critical than the others. They are, in no particular order:

Left Tackle: It takes (at least) five guys to protect the quarterback and the hardest guys to block are edge rushers, making both tackle spots important. Given that most quarterbacks are right-handed, they drop back to pass without being able to see what's going on to their left. This makes left tackle the premier position on the offensive line and, therefore, a premier position in the draft.

Defensive Line: The game is won and lost in the trenches and defense wins championships so the defensive line is extra important. If an offense wants to run, the best way to stop it is with a strong defensive line. If an offense wants to pass, the quickest way to stop them is with a strong defensive line. Sure, edge rushers are great at pressuring quarterbacks, but push up the middle from a stout line is the shortest path to the quarterback. It doesn't matter how good the rest of a defense is, if the defensive line is getting pushed around, opposing offenses will be able to march down the field without much of a problem.

Edge Rusher: These are the guys that wreak the most havoc on passers. Flying off the edge, they have the moves to get around tackles with a higher probability of getting to the quarterback as fast as possible. It's rare that a Pro-Bowl edge rusher is drafted after the first round and most of them go in the top 10 picks. This means that premier edge rushers are easily identified and almost always taken early, making them a prized position in the draft.

Cornerback: It's a passing league and, as much as defensive linemen and edge rushers help stop the pass, you still need guys to cover the receivers. Cornerbacks have to be fast enough to run with the fastest players in the game, agile enough to stick with them on hard-cut routes, disciplined enough to not bite on double moves and pump fakes, and have the mental fortitude to not flustered when they get beat or have a bad call go against them (because it happens to all of them).

NON-PREMIUM POSITIONS

There are also some positions that are... less premium. This does not make them unimportant, but they tend to be valued less in the draft for various reasons. If there is a terrible player on the field, the opposition will attack them, there's no way around that, but there are positions that are easier to get by with if a team doesn't have elite talent.

Interior Offensive Linemen: Guards have a tough job to do, blocking giant defensive linemen in close quarters where it's hard for refs to see all that dirty stuff, but they're doing it in tight space where they have their buddies close by to help, they don't have to worry about edge rushers taking a wide swooping arc around them, and they often have running backs to help pickup any defenders they miss.

Safety: Safeties aren't unimportant, but the fact of the matter is, if you have a good defensive line, good linebackers, and good cornerbacks, you will be just fine with pedestrian safeties back there.

Inside Linebackers: Sure, it's great to have a game-changer like Bobby Wagner on your team, but, like safety, if inside linebackers are surrounded with good talent, they can be the middle of the donut and the defense won't miss a beat. This doesn't make them unimportant, but it's easier for a defense to get by with average inside linebackers or safeties than with average edge rushers or cornerbacks.

SKILL POSITIONS

Oh boy, now we get to the shiny objects!

Running backs and (especially) wide receivers generate a lot of discussion on value. It's easy to see what game-breaking talent like Saquon Barkley or DeAndre Hopkins brings to the table in an offense, but are they worth high draft picks?

When you can find a wide receiver like Tyreek Hill or a running back like Aaron Jones in the 5th round, it starts to look like skill players are a little easier to find. The league leaders list each year certainly shows plenty of guys getting plenty of yards even if they weren't picked in the first round.

There's an abundance of skill players in every draft and I think it's systemic.

When these guys first started playing football at the park when they were kids, the best athletes wanted to score touchdowns. They play running back and wide receiver in school and by the time they go to a big college in Florida, that's what they're still doing. Overbearing football dads push their kids to be at the visible positions where their children's little egos can get all the positive reinforcement they can handle.

Participation trophies aren't enough-I've faced youth coaches that call a timeout with one second left when they're winning by multiple scores because they want to get another touchdown for one of their kids. This sends kids the message that scoring is king. None of those coaches ever called a timeout when they were on defense because they wanted to get one of their players another sack.

This doesn't stop at Pop Warner. When kids get to high school, they know that touchdowns get scholarships. When they're in college, the programs push offense. It sells tickets, it gets the alumni excited (hooray for boosters), and these guys get the girls-the head cheerleader is never checking out the left guard's foot leverage. No, the girls want Touchdown Boy.

At all these stages, top athletes gravitate towards and are pushed to play offense. As the old joke says: a wide receiver who can't catch is called a cornerback. Just look at Sam Shields. He had all the skills and ability to be a top-10 corner in the NFL, but because of his crazy athleticism, he was given nearly unlimited chances to be a wide receiver, even though he couldn't really do it. He only played cornerback for his final season in college and it was as a last resort, having exhausted every possible chance to play offense.

There are also physical limitations. Guys who are 5'9" like Steve Smith and Wes Welker can play wide receiver at a Pro Bowl level because of speed, quickness, and agility. It's much harder to play defense at that size. Guys that size usually just get run over.

All of these factors contribute to a nearly inexhaustible supply of wide receivers. The 2020 draft looks really deep at wide receiver... so did the 2019 draft... come to think of it, when was the last time a draft wasn't deep at wide receiver?

On top of that, when did a team ever win a Super Bowl on the strength of its premier first round wide receivers or running backs?

It's been a while.

As great as generational talents like Randy Moss, Calvin Johnson, Barry Sanders, and LaDainian Tomlinson were, they never got a ring.

Skill position players tend to be poor first round investments, as we'll explore later.

DRAFTING WITH POSITIONAL VALUE

That's a lot to take in, but it looks like a bunch of theories and examples.

How does this play out in real life? Should teams never take a guard or safety in the first round?

Maybe. Let's look at the recent history of how championship teams have been built.

I've charted this for a number of years on my website PackersForTheWin.com. Looking back at the Super Bowl winners for the 2012-2019 seasons, I mapped out what positions the winning team chose in the first round with their previous five years worth of drafts (or what position the pick was traded for in a couple cases). I chose five years because that's the contract length for first round picks on a cheap contract - this analysis shows what these teams focused on and what they were built around.

The results are as follows:

- 9 Defensive Linemen
- 8 Edge / Outside Linebacker
- 8 Trade Downs (out of the first round)
- 5 Offensive Linemen
- 4 Cornerbacks
- 4 Quarterbacks
- 1 Safety
- 1 Running Back
- 1 Wide Receiver
- 0 Inside Linebackers
- 0 Tight Ends

Notice how the teams that win the Super Bowl seem to focus on the positions I identified as premier? That's weird, huh? And one of the most popular options for these teams was to trade down and get additional value, something we talked about in the value-based approach to drafting.

What other conclusions can we draw here?

Apparently, if you want to win the Super Bowl in the next five years, you shouldn't waste your first round picks on tight ends or inside linebackers. This isn't a hard and fast rule, of course, but this trend definitely shows that those are considered luxury positions.

Inside linebacker is a luxury position because they are surrounded by their teammates. They can hide in the middle if the defense is set up right. As a result, they aren't as coveted and don't get drafted as high - Bobby Wagner and Darius Leonard, two All-Pro inside linebackers, were both drafted in the second round.

Tight end is a luxury position because they are a hybrid blocker-receiver. If you have good enough blockers and receivers, you might not need a dominant tight end. And because tight end is generally an undervalued position, like inside linebackers, good ones can be found later.

Tight end Rob Gronkowski, a 4-time First Team All-Pro and member of the NFL 100th Anniversary All-Time Team, was a 2nd round pick in 2010. The Raiders actually had Gronkowski rated as the best player in the draft, but still traded the pick to the Patriots because of how undervalued the position is.

All-Pro tight end George Kittle, the heir apparent to the title of Best Tight End In The League, was a 5th round pick in 2018. This is due in part to poor scouting, but there's no denying that his position is not valued.

Of course, none of this stopped the Lions from making tight end TJ Hockenson one of the highest-drafted tight ends of all time when they selected him with the 8th overall pick in the 2019 draft, but do you really want to be like the Lions?

Skill position players simply were not valued highly by teams that won Super Bowls over the last decade.

In addition to zero tight ends, these champions only took one wide receiver and one running back in the first round. Eight champions, each with five 1st round picks, and they only took two skill position players.

But would it have worked out if they had taken a safety or a tight end?

Would the Chiefs have won the Super Bowl if they had drafted an inside linebacker in the first round?

I don't know. No one knows. That's the nature of the draft. The best we can do is try to learn from history.

SPECIAL TEAMS

In addition to determining premier and non-premier positions on offense and defense, teams also have to worry about drafting special teams.

Let's start with the kickers and punters - they get all the attention.

One of the big questions about drafting these guys is when to take them. Going back to the principles of value-based drafting, they can be tough to differentiate.

In the 2019 NFL season, kickers made most of their extra points and the difference between a top 10 kicker and a bottom-of-the-barrel guy is only a few field goals, maybe a point per game.

As for punters, the difference between being ranked 2nd or 28th was less than 4 yards a kick. Yes, you want consistency from these guys, but it's hard to tell who's going to be consistent, and it's pretty easy to stay competitive with middling guys if you've drafted well on offense and defense.

Kicker and punter are also unique positions in that their jobs are more mentally stressful than physically demanding.

I'm not saying it's easy to kick a 50-yard field goal or boom a 60-yard punt, but there are a surprisingly high number of guys with the leg strength and form to do those things. The hard part of doing it in the NFL is the mental pressure. Even the strongest-legged veteran is susceptible to a shank in crunch time. The margin of error for a 50-yard field is 3.54 degrees in either direction.

Three. Point. Five. Four. Degrees.

Think about that.

Look at how silly a football is shaped. Look at what football cleats look like. A 3.54 degree angle is incredibly small when you think of those two things clashing with each other.

That's why the mental aspect of kicking is so critical. It's also why coaches ice kickers but not any other positions.

No matter how good a kicker is, it's hard to separate yourself from the pack when the margin of error is so small.

As for punters, their impact is limited by other factors. They need a good coverage team to keep any of their yards and if the offense has moved the ball even a little past the typical starting point of the 25-yard line, they won't be able to use all their leg strength, anyway.

These are all the reasons why teams rarely spend high picks on specialists. Only three kickers have ever been selected in the first round and only two punters.

The most recent example of a high choice spent on a specialist was in 2016 when the Buccaneers selected FSU kicker Roberto Aguayo in the second round. In his rookie year, he had the worst field goal percentage in the league and was cut. He never played again.

Teams don't want to mess around taking a specialist that high when the failure rate is astronomical and the best possible reward is a guy who's just a little better than the median.

Where special teams drafting really starts to get interesting is in the last couple of rounds.

NFL rosters are only 53 players and only 46 of them are active on games. When you have more than half of them playing regular snaps on offense and defense, you need some other guys to play special teams.

Those slots usually fall to the younger players towards the bottom of the roster, which makes for some interesting decisions in the late rounds: do you go for a guy with a very tiny chance of contributing at his position, or do you try to get guys who could be good special teams players?

If you want guys who are good special teams players, you need to evaluate players for those traits. Odds are, most of your scouting is going to be of those guys playing offense and defense, making player evaluation even more difficult.

10

WHY GMS DO STUPID THINGS

B ecoming an NFL GM is extremely difficult. There are only 32 positions like it in the world and it's one of the tiny handful of jobs that will pay you millions of dollars to talk football all day.

Getting one of these jobs is next to impossible.

Once someone gets one of those 32 highly coveted jobs, they tend to do anything they can to keep it.

The best way to keep that job?

Win.

The quickest way to lose that job?

Lose.

Guess what? Teams that don't have a good quarterback usually lose.

Teams win without good running backs or receivers. Teams win with bad safeties or mediocre linebackers. Heck, teams even win with nondescript offensive lines or cornerbacks.

But teams don't win with bad quarterbacks.

Trent Dilfer, the Ravens quarterback in their 2000 Super Bowl winning season is a lightning rod for discussions involving the importance of quarterbacks. He is often (unfairly, in my eyes) brought up as the worst quarterback ever to win a Super Bowl.

Here's the deal though: Trent Dilfer was a First Team All-American in college with the talent to be drafted #6 overall. He was good enough to make a Pro Bowl and last 13 years in the NFL.

The Ravens were 5-3 before Trent Dilfer took over as the starting quarterback. He lost his first start by a field goal against the division rival Steelers after leading at the half. After that, he led the team to 11 straight wins (where the team averaged over 26 points per game after averaging only 9 points per game in the four games before he took over), including the Super Bowl.

That's it.

That's the "worst" quarterback ever to win a Super Bowl.

A First Team All-American, #6 overall, Pro-Bowl quarterback that took over a team and started tripling their offensive output.

Tell that to your friends the next time they say the Ravens won a Super Bowl with a bad quarterback.

Let this serve as undeniable proof that an NFL team can't win with a bad quarterback.

Now, herein lies the problem. This is how bad football teams can get stuck in a cycle of losing.

Let's say a team has a bad quarterback and loses. They fire their GM (after all, it's their fault they don't have a good quarterback, right?). Now a new GM comes in and inherits a mess (it's actually pretty rare for teams that are doing great to fire their GM and bring in a new guy).

The new GM is trying to clean up the mess, but it takes time. After a couple years, the owner starts getting antsy for a championship (let's face it, most owners are just fans who made a ton of money in another business - they want to win and they view the GM as the person responsible for it).

The GM wonders if he will have a job if next season doesn't go well. Looking at his quarterback, he comes to the conclusion that things won't go well next year unless they upgrade the position.

If teams have a good quarterback, they usually won't trade him away or let him leave as a free agent.

That leaves the draft.

Unfortunately, in this example, as bad as the team was in the previous season, they weren't the worst team in the league. They have a high draft pick, but not high enough to get one of the top quarterback prospects (since quarterbacks always get drafted so high).

So what does he do? He tries to trade up.

But other bad teams are also trying to trade up, so he has to make a bold move. He trades the team's 1st round picks for the next three years so he can move up and take a QB in the top 3.

It seems reactionary from an analyst's perspective. It seems like a foolish move, even cowardly, from a fan's perspective.

But let's look at it from the GM's perspective.

If the GM makes the bold, all-in move we just described, what are the possible outcomes?

1. The QB is great, the team does better, and the GM looks brilliant (and, more importantly, keeps his job).
2. The QB flops, he looks like an idiot, and he loses his job... which he was going to lose anyway since he didn't have a good QB (sure, the team is hamstrung for the next few years because of the draft picks he traded away, but that's not his problem anymore - let the next GM worry about that! It sounds harsh and inconsiderate, but it is absolutely the nature of this job).
3. Any middle ground where he keeps his job is also an acceptable outcome to the GM.

It doesn't take a deep analysis of the alternatives to see why GMs make moves like this.

A look back at how some of the trades to move up for a quarterback have gone down in recent years can tell us a lot about the best way to handle the situation.

11

DRAFT CASE STUDIES

Histoy is the best teacher when it comes to the draft. There's a lot to be learned by looking back to see how bold moves have worked out for teams in the past.

Redskins Trade Up for Robert Griffin III in 2012

In 2011, the Redskins went 5-11 with Rex Grossman (who had 1 win as a starting quarterback in the previous 3 seasons combined). Bruce Allen was in his second year as General Manager and very much wanted to have a third. He knew they needed a change.

The Redskins did bad enough to "earn" the 6th overall pick, but the draft class's top two quarterbacks (Andrew Luck and Robert Griffin III) weren't going to last that long.

Allen made the bold move of trading their 1st and 2nd round picks, along with their 1st round picks the next *two* years, to the Rams for the #2 overall pick, which they used on Robert Griffin III.

Griffin won Rookie of the Year honors, then blew out his knee in the playoffs. He went 3-10 the following year and has been a backup ever since.

The Rams traded down with many of the picks and ended up with three 1st round picks, two 2nd round picks, a 3rd round pick, and a 6th round pick.

If they'd kept those picks, and drafted wisely, they could have got Russell Wilson as their quarterback and still had the draft picks to select Chandler Jones, Bobby Wagner, Le'Veon Bell, David Bakhtiari, *and* Aaron Donald.

Instead, they got one good year, one bad knee, and a lot of regret.

Bears Trade Up For Mitch Trubisky in 2017

The Bears finished 2016 at 3-13 in Ryan Pace's first year as General Manager. He knew his second year would have to be better if he wanted there to be a third year.

Matt Barkley, Jay Cutler, and Brian Hoyer took turns starting in 2016, with each earning one victory. Pace was smart enough to know that wasn't going to cut it in 2017.

The Bears were all the way up at #3 in the 2017 draft and the class featured three quarterbacks that scouts had rated as worthy of high picks: Patrick Mahomes, Deshaun Watson, and Mitch Trubisky.

Pace could have stayed at #3 and been guaranteed one of them.

When the Browns took defensive end Myles Garrett at

#1 overall, the Bears knew they would have a choice between at least two of the three big quarterbacks in the class.

That wasn't good enough for Pace. He's smart enough to know that you can't take risks at the quarterback position. He wanted *his* guy.

Pace sent his 3rd and 4th round picks to the 49ers to move up from #3 overall to #2 overall to make darn sure that no one else jumped ahead of him to take his guy.

The 49ers ended up taking defensive end Solomon Thomas.

Wait a minute - that's not a quarterback!

Did the Bears get duped by the 49ers!?

Not necessarily.

Even though the 49ers (who had recently moved on from Colin Kaepernick and would soon trade for quarterback Jimmy Garoppolo) apparently had no interest in taking a quarterback at #2 ahead of the Bears, it was very possible that another team could trade up instead and take the player that Pace coveted.

The player Pace coveted was Mitchell Trubisky.

After taking over the starting job from Mike Glennon a month into his rookie season, Trubisky showed signs of growth. He led them to a division title in 2018, before regressing to 8-8 the following year, while Watson and Mahomes have fared far better.

The 49ers took Solomon Thomas at #3 and he has been a role player for an absolutely monstrous defensive front. They traded away the 3rd pick to the Saints, who used it on Pro-Bowl running back Alvin Kamara, while the 4th round pick was not far from where the best tight end in the league, George Kittle, was selected.

So, the Bears got Mitch Trubisky instead of Patrick Mahomes, Alvin Kamara, and George Kittle.

LESSONS

Why did the Redskins and Bears fare so poorly in these debacles?

Injuries played a part in the Redskins folly, but even if Griffin had stayed healthy, he would have had a hard time out-producing the value that could have come from Russell Wilson and the cast of all-stars that could have been taken with those picks.

If you really dive into the stories, you'll find two big factors at work in these debacles:

1. Poor scouting
2. Desperation for a QB

Scouting is scouting and when it's bad, it's bad.

Taking Robert Griffin III over Russell Wilson is bad scouting. Taking Mitch Trubisky over Patrick Mahomes and Deshaun Watson is really bad scouting.

There will be misses like that, no way around it. You try to learn from it and get better at scouting.

But when you throw desperation into the mix and make a desperate trade, you're just pouring gasoline on a dumpster fire.

We know that bad drafting decisions will be made even with really good scouts doing the best they can.

However, teams can still do their best by not taking desperate measures.

What if the Bears let someone else trade with the 49ers for the #2 overall pick? Maybe if they sat tight, another team would have moved up for Trubisky and they could have got "stuck" with Patrick Mahomes.

What if the Redskins would have stayed at #6 overall and taken Luke Kuechly or Stephon Gilmore? Maybe they wait until the 3rd round and take Russell Wilson six picks before the Seahawks?

Let's actually look a little more at that Russell Wilson selection.

Why didn't the Seahawks take a quarterback earlier than the 3rd round? They actually traded down in the 1st round (moving down three spots to pick up an extra 4th and 6th round pick).

Why?

Earlier in the offseason, they had signed Matt Flynn to a reasonable free agent deal to be their starting quarterback. They were in no hurry to find a new quarterback, but thought Wilson had enough potential to warrant taking him in the 3rd round.

What about the Chiefs when they drafted Patrick Mahomes? They had Alex Smith as a starter. He'd won 22 games for them over the previous two years and was a reigning Pro Bowler.

The Chiefs weren't scrambling in desperation. They traded up when they saw Mahomes fall, but they did it on their terms from a position of bargaining power. If the Chiefs hadn't had a Pro-Bowl quarterback on their roster, you had better believe that teams would have charged more for them to move up.

Look at some other good moves that teams have made by exhibiting patience in the process.

The Packers took Aaron Rodgers at #24 overall in 2005. Many people thought Rodgers had the talent to go number #1 overall. If the Packers were desperate for a quarterback, they may have tried to trade up. They weren't desperate, though - they still had Brett Favre, who played six more seasons. The Packers landed Rodgers because they weren't acting out of desperation. They took the value that fell to them.

Go back even further and look at Tom Brady. The Patriots stole him in the 6th round of the 2000 draft. What were they doing waiting so long to draft a quarterback? Well, they already had Drew Bledsoe, who had led them to the Super Bowl a few years prior. The Patriots could afford to be patient in looking for their next quarterback because they already had one (they also took a swing on a late-round quarterback the year before when they drafted Michael Bishop, again showing thier patience in looking for value).

The best time to get a quarterback is when you already have one and aren't desperate.

But if you already have a quarterback, you don't need one and drafting one won't help you win now.

It's quite the quandary for GMs, but history shows that waiting patiently to find good value almost always outweighs big "all-in" trades to move up.

This usually comes up in regard to quarterbacks, but

it's true for every position. Let's look at a case study that doesn't involve a quarterback.

2011 Falcons trade up for Julio Jones

We know that skill positions are easy to get in later rounds. We know that wide receivers are just big shiny objects.

Even still, some NFL GMs (who probably didn't read this book) hear the siren song of the wide receiver.

The Falcons had posted winning seasons three years in a row and finished 2010 with a 13-3 record that had their young quarterback Matt Ryan looking like a star in the making. After a disappointing loss to the Packers in the playoffs, General Manager Thomas Dimitroff thought his team was just one big playmaker away from winning it all.

The problem was they were picking all the way down at #27 and the two big wide receiver prospects in the class - AJ Green and Julio Jones - were sure to be gone by then.

After the Bengals selected Green with the 4th overall pick (a move that, spoiler alert, did not get them to the Super Bowl), the Falcons made a bold move to jump up for Jones.

The Falcons gave up their 1st, 2nd, and 4th round picks in 2011 plus their 1st and 4th round picks in 2012 to take Julio Jones... a wide receiver. Remember when I said wide receivers aren't premier positions? Well, how many Super Bowls did Julio Jones win? The same number as Randy Moss, the same number as Calvin Johnson.

He was the best receiver in the game, but was he worth it?

Remember that adage we discussed earlier that says defense wins championships? Let's imagine the Falcons held on to all those picks and focused on defense instead. With those choices, they could have drafted defensive end Cameron Heyward, linebacker Justin Houston, cornerback Richard Sherman, safety Harrison Smith, and cornerback Josh Norman.

That's five All-Pro defenders.

Now, maybe the Falcons offense would have suffered a little, but what if half of their defense was made up of All-Pros? What if they had Cam Heyward and Justin Houston rushing the quarterback while Richard Sherman and Josh Norman clamped down receivers and Harrison Smith roamed the back end?

Could that have had more of an impact than a single wide receiver, even one as good as Julio Jones?

Absolutely. No question.

I think Julio Jones was the best receiver in the game, but it's still foolish to use a 1st round pick on a wide receiver.

Using a premium top 6 pick on a receiver is just ridiculous.

Giving up what the Falcons gave up to get one is absolutely bonkers.

LESSONS

What can we learn from this?

The same things we learned from our quarterback case studies: desperation and drafting don't mix.

The Falcons could have sat tight and picked absolute

studs for their defense. If they really thought they needed a wide receiver, they could have stayed where they were and still got Pro-Bowl wide receivers like Randall Cobb, Alshon Jeffery, and TY Hilton without giving up the bounty of valuable picks that they did.

Wide receivers usually aren't good value in the earliest portion of the draft and big moves up the board rarely net as much value as simply staying put and drafting better would.

In 2011, the Falcons showed us what happens when you do both.

12

EXERCISE

I f your curiosity has been piqued and you still want to understand the draft a little better, I'd encourage you to do this (seemingly) simple exercise in preparation for the draft.

Find an online mock draft simulator and run a mock draft while you make the selections for your favorite team. Learn a little bit about the players, see who you think would be a good fit, balancing team needs with value and matching them against your assessment of the players.

Then do another mock draft the next day... and the next. Just do one mock draft each day until the actual draft. It can take as little time as you want, but I think you'll enjoy it the most if you look up a couple new players each day.

If you do this every day, you'll notice that the boards start to shift after the Senior Bowl and they change again after the Scouting Combine - teams and analysts put a lot of stock into these events and the results will really rock the boards.

Then, when the big event comes, when the actual draft happens and your team comes up, jot down who you would take. Share it on social media or document it somewhere private (I actually do both).

Then, at the end of the year, go back and see how you stacked up.

Do this again next year, and the following year. Revisit your results from years ago to see how you did and what you learned.

If you're interested in football enough to read this book, I think you'll get a lot of entertainment from this exercise.

Happy drafting.

13

WRAP UP

Professional football is the most popular sport in America, it's the ultimate reality television show. The NFL draft is an incredibly complex process and by far the most entertaining draft of any major sport.

I hope you've enjoyed this look into many of the aspects that make it so compelling and dramatic. I hope you've gained a better understanding of the multitude of issues that make drafting such a difficult process for NFL GMs.

Most of all, I hope this book gave you a better understanding of how the draft works, appreciate how difficult it is, and enjoy it more as a result.

If you'd like to see more of my draft coverage, feel free to follow me on Twitter at @PackersForTheWn or check out my website at PackersForTheWin.com.

THANK YOU

Thank you for reading!

I truly hoped you enjoyed delving deeper into NFL Draft strategy.

If you enjoyed this book, would you please consider leaving a five-star review? This link will take you to the page:

PackersForTheWin.com/ReviewDraft

Reviews are the lifeblood of any book. Your review can help others find this book, in addition supporting me.

Thank you so much,

-Bruce

ABOUT THE AUTHOR

Bruce Irons is a fan of football who has watched, played, coached, studied, and thoroughly enjoyed the sport for decades.

You can read more of his analysis at:
PackersForTheWin.com

You can also follow him on Twitter:
@BruceIronsNFL

BOOKS BY BRUCE IRONS

A Fan's Guide To Understanding The NFL Draft: Strategies, Tactics, And Case Studies For Building A Professional Football Team

A Fan's Guide To NFL Free Agency Hits And Misses: Case Studies And Lessons From Landmark Signings Throughout History

A Fan's Guide To Understanding The NFL Salary Cap: How The NFL Salary Cap Works And Why It Matters

GLOSSARY

A list of terms sure to be thrown around during draft coverage.

Anticipation: This is like a sixth sense for football players - it's knowing what is going to happen before it happens. A player with good anticipation could refer to a quarterback who understands how a receiver will run a route and how the defender will react (allowing him to throw the ball before the receiver is looking and still hit him), a running back who intuitively understands where holes will open up as the offensive linemen and defensive linemen are crashing into each other (allowing him to run to the spot with perfect timing and not waste any stutter steps trying to get through the line), or a defensive back who understands where a receiver's route will lead him and where the quarterback is likely to throw the ball (allowing him to break up the pass or intercept the ball).

Ball Skills: The ability to see a ball in the air, run

under it at a pace that keeps the defender at bay, and catch it before anyone else can.

Base (or Power Base): Usually refers to an offensive or defensive lineman; this is a player's ability to stand his ground when someone else is trying to push him around.

Burst: The ability to come up to speed quickly with full power.

Change of Direction: Moving full speed in one direction and able to quickly move in a different direction. This is helpful for linebackers when defending a running back that makes quick cuts and helpful for defensive backs to guard receivers on double moves.

Change of Pace Back: A running back who has a unique skill set, but is not considered a full-time player. This is usually a small, quick back who can't stand up to the pounding of 20 carries per game, but provides value by making defenses deal with another unique skill set.

Ceiling: The draft word for potential. Guys with a high ceiling have a lot of potential, while guys with a low ceiling are usually considered to be at or near their potential and probably won't get much better than they already are.

Circus Elephant: A big guy who is really agile and able to move.

Deep Threat: A receiver who is generally very fast and can get downfield faster than his defender.

Delivery: Refers to a quarterback's mechanics when he throws the ball. For example, if he doesn't bring his elbow up, he may have more balls batted down at the line.

Fluid Hips: A player with fluid hips can change direction very easily, like a cornerback that is running laterally with a receiver, but needs to quickly turn around and keep running at full speed to keep up with a change in route.

High Character: A player you hope you won't have to worry about getting arrested.

Late Riser: A player that was rated higher as the draft got closer. This can because he finished his last season with a flourish, had good Senior Bowl practices, or performed well at the Combine.

Motor: The energy level a player exhibits. A high-motor guy gives his all every play and doesn't seem to get tired.

Possession Receiver: A receiver that is good at short to medium routes and has good hands, but usually lacks the speed to be a deep threat.

Pad Level: Refers to how high or low a player's shoulder pads are at contact, which plays into the leverage a player can get. Players with low pad level generally can move guys with high pad level (think back to levers and fulcrums in high school science class).

Polish: A "polished" player is one who has already refined his techniques and should require less coaching on the little things at the pro level. An unpolished receiver might have a stutter step when he breaks on his routes and an unpolished defensive tackle might need to change his elbow angles when he's working on his hand placement techniques.

Processing: Refers to how quickly a player can take in what is happening and make adjustments at game speed. A defensive lineman who is a quick processor can start off driving upfield to rush the passer, realize that the offensive line is trying to open a hole with run blocking techniques, and quickly shift his eyes and weight to get after the running back.

Project: A player that will take a lot of coaching and work to reach his potential, with no guarantees that he ever will. Project players are usually not taken until the mid to late rounds and fans will get mad if their favorite team takes a project in the first round.

Raw: A player that is still learning the game, typically someone who started playing football later in life (in pro terms, starting in high school can be considered late as most of these guys have been playing since grade school).

Read Option Quarterback: The read-option play (sometimes referred to as Read Pass Option or RPO) is a play where the quarterback gets the ball and hands it out where the running back can get it. Then, in a split second, the QB reads the defense to see if he wants to actually hand off the ball, run it himself, or pull it back for a pass. Quarterbacks have to be mentally and physically quick to run this type of offense, but it can drive defenses mad because it's incredibly hard to defend when you don't know what's coming until the last possible moment.

Red Flag: Anything that causes concern about a player from an injury red flag (wondering if he will get hurt a lot or if he will recover from an injury he currently has) to character concerns (wondering if he will get into legal troubles or be suspended).

Release Point: Where the quarterback's hand is when he lets go of the ball on a pass. Typically, this should be when his arm is at the top of its motion. If the release point comes too early or too late, the ball will lack full power and accuracy.

Set The Edge: Refers to defensive ends and outside linebackers moving upfield to make it difficult (hopefully impossible) for backs to run around them toward the sideline.

Shutdown Corner: A cornerback who can line up on a receiver and shut him down, instead of being relegated to playing zone defense or needing help from a safety to cover the best receiver

Sleeper: A player that you think will be better than most other people think or even a player that other people haven't heard of.

Tweener: A player that could play multiple positions but doesn't seem to dominate one or the other. This often refers to an offensive lineman that could play guard or tackle or a defender than could play defensive end or outside linebacker or edge rusher.

Waist Bend: This is a bad thing for linemen. It means they don't bend their knees and square their shoulders to get good leverage. Instead, they just bend over. In college, physically dominant players can get away with this against lesser opponents, but if they don't correct the flaws in their form, they usually don't make it in the pros, where tougher competition will destroy them.

Made in the USA
Monee, IL
23 July 2022